Positive Thinking Workbook

2 Months of Creative Journal Ideas

No.1 Amazon Bestselling Author
Veena N. Rutherford

Copyright

Introduction

A fun and interactive journal that contains 2 months of different and interactive writing prompts to promote positive thinking and kick start the law of attraction in your favor.

Discover more about yourself as you answer the questions and begin your journey of self-exploration. The questions are fun, unique and really get you thinking about the things you love, the things you have yet to discover and where your life is heading. You will learn more about yourself and learn things about yourself you never even realized you would.

Remember:

"...The Mind is Everything. What You Think, You Become..." - Buddha

Most importantly, as well as gaining a deeper understanding of your inner-self, at the same time you will be attracting your dream life in your direction, one step at a time!

So get yourself comfortable, grab a warm, comforting drink and settle into your favorite chair and start your journey towards making your dreams a reality...

"...I am in control of my emotions. Today I choose happiness..."

Describe your dream life in 100 words or less

List **10** things you want to achieve before you are **100** years old

Draw a picture of your dream home

(p.s – even if you are not Picasso, you can still scribble something that will make sense to you and help you visualize it!)

List your **10** favorite things in the world

(p.s – this can be colors, foods, objects, jewelry, textures, locations etc. The only limit is your imagination!)

What are you grateful for in your home life?

List your 5 favorite possessions

What is your best memory?

What possession are you hoarding unnecessarily?

(p.s - list it, then get rid of it - you'll feel better afterwards!)

What do you want most right now? List 3 ways you can make it happen

Name your favorite compliment

List your 5 favorite attributes

What are you best at?

What gets you most enthusiastic?

What would you want to achieve if fear wasn't holding you back?

(p.s - eliminate your fear — and then you will be surprised at how much easier this goal is!)

What would you do today, if you knew no one would judge you?

What has been your best compliment to date?

What have you done to help yourself achieve your dream life lately? (if the answer is "nothing", then go do something right away, then write it down here!)

What is the bravest thing you have ever done?

Are my fears real or are they all imagined?

(p.s - list your fears and mark next to each one how "real" it is - they may just be in your head!)

What is the worst that could happen when striving to achieve my goals?

(p.s – if it isn't that bad , then go for it!)

What is the point in worrying?

(p.s – try to list 3 ways worrying helps you. When you can't think of any good ones, then you will realize that worrying about nothing is a waste of time!)

Name 1 time you were happy for someone else's success

(p.s – being happy for someone else will force good energy to flow through you, allowing your own dreams to come true!)

List 3 ways you can help someone today

Name something unexpected that happened recently and how you can put a positive slant on it

List 5 successes you have had ever in your life

What 3 happy memories do you want to create in the next year?

Forget about what you have lost - name 3 things you have gained in the last 3 months

What is the one thing you are most grateful for in your life?

Name 1 time a bad experience turned into a good one

What aspects of your life do you enjoy the most?

Which aspects of your life would you most like to change?

When was the last time you went a whole day without complaining about anything? Can you do that tomorrow?

What are the most important 3 lessons life has taught you so far?

How can you use your talents to achieve your goals?

(p.s – everyone has something they are good at, even if they don't know it yet!)

You are successful if you are able to recover from failure, name 3 times you have done that and what you did to fix things

Name 10 times you said "I can" or "I can't" and you turned out to be exactly right? What can you learn from these occasions?

What new things did you learn yesterday?

What new gifts were you given in the last 3 months?

What are you grateful for in your love life?

What has been your most proud achievement to date?

(p.s - this can be anything, even if it was something you did back in school!)

What are you grateful for in your work life?

List your 5 favorite people in the world
(p.s - if you are not one of them, then you should be!)

What was the most fun thing you ever did?

(p.s – arrange to go it more often!)

List 5 things you should be grateful for in your life, even if they were not quite as you expected them to be

Is it true that you compliment people more than you criticize them?
(p.s - if not then change it - your miracle will be more likely to happen then!)

"You cannot stop a river, but you can learn how to swim." How can you "learn to swim" in your everyday life to break down the barriers that are holding you back from your goals?

What will you do tomorrow to make yourself happy?

What has your favorite experience been so far? How can you make it happen again?

List 5 ways you can get your dream house (p.s - even if they seem "wacky" write them down anyway - anything is possible!)

"If you can dream it, then you can do it." List 3 things you can daydream about in the next week that you want to happen

List 3 things you can do today to make yourself happy

(p.s – this could cooking your favorite meal, going to your favorite place or listening to your favorite album)

Tomorrow is a chance to start a new life. What will you do on your first day?

Name 3 ways you are closer to achieving you goal this year than you were last year

Describe your positive features in 10 words

List 10 things you would like to say "yes" to

Describe a time when you felt really satisfied

If you could send a
message to your
younger self, it would
be...

List 5 things that make you smile

My ideal day would be spent...

What is the most inspirational movie you have watched?

65093540R00037

Made in the USA
Lexington, KY
30 June 2017